Cottages in the Sun

Bungalows of Venice, California

Introduction

A playful color scheme dresses up this simple cottage, signaling the imaginative possibilities for embellishing one's own home.

Creativity is embedded in the DNA of Venice, California. The beachside community at the westernmost edge of the City of Los Angeles has long been known as a fertile ground for the arts and for lifestyle innovation. Even at its inception more than a century ago, when visionary entrepreneur Abbot Kinney built his Venice-of-America with its network of canals and fanciful buildings, the cultural aspirations of this seaside resort were high—if not long-lived.

This aura of fantasy and imaginative possibility has somehow endured over the years as integral to the zeitgeist of the place. And today, that spirit finds expression in a multitude of ways—in art, in architecture, in fashion, and in leisure—that have emerged from this incubator of the avant-garde. The energy of Venice continues to draw thousands, even millions, to its public spaces—the famed boardwalk, a destination for visitors from around the world; the canals, or what remains of them; and the lively Abbot Kinney Boulevard, with its boutiques, galleries, cafes, and restaurants.

Yet it is along the intimate walk streets and avenues, and in small pockets along the canals, that one can catch glimpses of another and less well-known dimension of this dynamic community: the vintage bungalows and cottages of Venice's past. Stalwart survivors of the ebb and flow of the area's fortunes, these small homes channel the creative spirit of the place and provide a welcome counterpoint to the oversized, lot-filling modernist boxes that increasingly populate the area's often ragged but desirable neighborhoods.

Cottages—cool and hot and green

The styles and sensibilities of these homes vary widely, reflecting the eclectic nature of architecture in Venice itself. The point of departure might be a simple early-twentieth-century gabled cottage, a modest Craftsman or Spanish bungalow, or even a small postwar tract house. And then the adventure begins.

Color, landscape, treasured collections, personal narrative, contemporary overlays and additions, art and craft, and inventive design all combine in various ways to produce domestic environments with unique and deeply personal points of view. The 28 homes showcased in the following pages are one-of-a-kind places that one owner aptly calls "temples for living."

The process is a dynamic one. These vintage homes, by their very nature, are often works in progress, evolving, like life itself. Old and new are, by necessity and intent, in constant dialogue, responding to the way we live now.

Common strategies emerge, such as removing walls where possible to create open floor plans in which living, dining, and kitchen areas connect; raising ceilings to enhance the

Capturing the eclectic, creative spirit of Venice, a repurposed door framed by a casual profusion of oranges serves as a gate to a private front garden.

sense of space, especially critical in the smallest of the cottages; and inserting skylights to naturally illuminate dark interiors. Ingenuity is applied to every nook and cranny to maximize the potential of each square inch where space is at a premium. Renovations also focus on creating new connections between inside and out, with added doors, windows, and decks to extend living into the garden, so much a part of the Southern California lifestyle.

The ethic of sustainability is also embedded in these homes. The mere act of preservation and renewal, rather than demolition and replacement, is the first gesture toward living green. Add to this the practice, employed in many of these homes, of incorporating recycled and repurposed materials, and you have "reduced, reused and recycled," a small but significant step toward the green revolution.

Connecting—to history and community

There are other dimensions to the process of the shaping of one's own vintage home. Owners become deeply invested in the ongoing narrative of their house, connecting to the particular history of what came before and forging, in the process, a sense of the house's future. Stewardship is a term often applied to major architectural or historical landmarks, but it applies equally to the preservation and renewal of the vernacular and the everyday, the true components of the fabric of neighborhoods that evolve over time. In such neighborhoods, scale and architectural character define a landscape that cannot be duplicated by even the most skilled designer, the New Urbanists notwithstanding.

This sense of stewardship, of personal investment, contributes to a feeling of community. Neighbors know and look out for one another. Longtime residents, newcomers, families, couples, singles, gays, and straights are all invested in the rich social fabric that defines a community. Whenever possible, residents walk to their destinations or use their bicycles. They borrow, free of charge, the vistas of adjacent gardens and landscapes to enrich their own sense of place. The search for meaning and beauty in a large metropolitan area can reside in one's own backyard, however small.

Creating a model

What can we learn from the cottages and bungalows of Venice?

Real estate trendspotters report a growing interest in the small home, dubbed the "newest cottage industry," as American culture moves away from super-size-me McMansions and toward a more balanced, sustainable approach to living and consumption. Venice residents speak of the liberation that comes with living in small spaces—of how downsizing allows individuals and families to focus on the essentials. This is a lesson that has a timely resonance.

"Small" is a word that need not apply to aspirations and ideas. The bungalows and cottages of Venice demonstrate, in no uncertain terms, that "small is not less, and conversely, big is not more," as one resident puts it. There is plenty of room here for creativity, for innovation, and for living the good life.

Cottage Reimagined

The dramatic purple spikes of Pride of Madeira mark the entrance to landscape architect Zack Freedman's canal-facing cottage. Bamboo fence by T. Rivas Rash II.

A Storied Place

John and Mary Sheller's 1906 bungalow comes with a special pedigree: local lore suggests that it was built by Venice founder Abbot Kinney for his son. Over the years, its occupants have ranged from circus folk—twin albino bareback riders, as the story goes—to bed-and-breakfast entrepreneurs, all pursuing their particular life journeys.

Their own life journey is what led the Shellers to the house in 2002, when, as empty nesters, they bought it "on a whim," trading their life in a "pleasant but boring neighborhood" for an adventure in the heart of Venice. The siting of the house was ideal: a stone's throw from the beach and the famed Venice

LEFT
A cottage-inspired garden leads to the steeply pitched gable entry of this Venice original, located on a walk street just steps from the boardwalk.

ABOVE
The front garden features several seating areas, including a secluded corner terrace bordered by a broken concrete wall.

LEFT
The formal living room sets the stage for the home's color palette of red, white, and blue. Light from the entryway is visible through the doorway, as is the original stairway leading to the second floor.

BOTTOM LEFT
The informal dining area and adjacent den (visible through the pass-through cabinet) were added during the expansion of the vintage house. Country-inspired furnishings and built-ins offer a sense of history.

boardwalk, and located on one of the original walk streets in a neighborhood layered with history.

An unusually large lot by Venice standards—40 feet x 120 feet—allowed the couple to consider extending the footprint of the two-story house toward the rear. They engaged architect Michael Hricak to chart the expansion plan: adding a reconfigured kitchen and den downstairs, and a guest suite, mezzanine, and roof deck upstairs. At the same time, they were careful to preserve many of the house's distinctive original features and profile, such as the front door and porch, the original inglenook in the living room, the old stairway, and the distinctive deep roof gables and rafter tails.

Inside, furnishings and colors reflect the Shellers' love of tradition and color, inspired by a mix of American Cottage, English Country, and the design aesthetic of Carl Larsson, "whose work we consulted often in our decisions," notes John. Children's book illustrations collected by John over many years, along with family art, grace the walls and offer a nostalgic and often fanciful touch to this carefully composed, well-organized interior.

Achieving this perfectly ordered domestic world took some doing, and more than a little bit of patience. The couple bravely occupied

the house throughout the two-year renovation, and today look back with a genuine appreciation for not only the results but also the skills and dedication of those who were instrumental in the process. They are quick to praise the painters, who spent four months stripping layers of paint, preparing surfaces, and finally applying the paint itself to create the bright, fresh feel of their rooms, readying them for the couple's favorite furniture, antiques, books, and art.

In the end, it all adds up to a place full of meaning, memory, and warm association. "This house is a good metaphor for our more than 30 years of marriage," says John. "We kept the best stuff, and tossed what we didn't need or want."

"With our move to Venice, we now have real live people with names and faces for neighbors, daily ocean breezes and crashing waves at night, yoga and restaurants, our beautiful walk street and its one hundred years of history. We have participated in the history of Venice by ensuring our house will stand another one hundred years."
— John Sheller

The walls of the house feature framed pieces from John Sheller's children's book illustration collection. In the den hangs one of the most recognizable: the cover of *Charlotte's Web* by Garth Williams.

IF THE SUN & MOON SHOULD DOUBT
THEY'D IMMEDIATELY GO OUT

TOP LEFT
The new second-floor guest suite features a quote from William Blake above the window seat that looks westward to the Pacific.

BOTTOM LEFT
Overlooking the guest suite, a small mezzanine, with its day bed, leads to the roof deck.

RIGHT
The new roof deck offers an expansive vista to the Pacific.

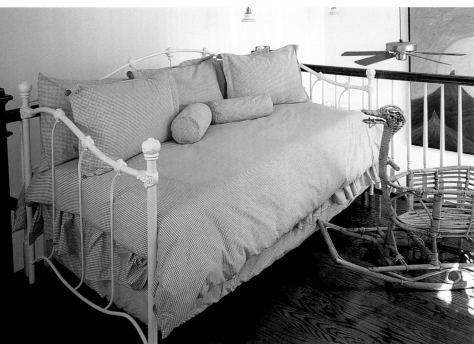

Designs on the Past

It was an unheard-of combination in Venice—a small street-facing cottage perched at the edge of a large corner lot, newly listed for sale. Built in 1889 in an as-yet unnamed rural outpost of Los Angeles, the house was reported to be the oldest structure in the Venice area still standing.

Indeed, it was standing, but just barely, when Katerina Tana happened upon it on her first day of house-hunting in 2000. Despite the fact that the cottage was considered a teardown, she was determined to revive and renew both it and the garden. Her intention sealed the deal with the sellers, a family that had occupied the property for the previous 70 years.

ABOVE
A rustic, whitewashed fence defines the entrance to the simple cottage, with its clapboard siding and single-gabled roof. Visible to the left, the same architectural language carries over to the new two-story accessory building, a garage and studio.

RIGHT
Slate flooring and spare, organic accents offer a decidedly contemporary take on the traditional front porch—a favorite place for relaxation.

In the intense nine months that followed, Tana—with a team of builders—uncovered the cottage's essence while updating it and making it her own. "I didn't want to lose the simplicity, the essential modesty of the place," says Tana, a designer and principal of her own firm. Yet she saw the potential in reworking the floor plan to create a greater feeling of openness and flow in the 1,000-square-foot structure. She combined rooms, raised the ceilings from eight to nine feet, and introduced skylights. To establish a stronger connection to the outdoors, she built a new side deck overlooking what was to become her expansive garden and outdoor living area. At the same time, she enhanced the cottage's original character-defining features, including its welcoming, generous front porch.

Inside, the cottage exudes a sophisticated, yet casual, global embrace—and reveals itself as a microcosm of her life experiences. With roots in Los Angeles, Tana grew up in London and has traveled the world. Drawing from a family history that traces to early Hollywood, middle and southern Europe, Tana's design sensibility channels experience and heritage to infuse her environment with deep personal meaning.

Every object counts. Whether a collection
of shells artfully arranged on a tabletop, or an
array of Turkish hand-painted tiles, there is
much to please the eye. Color, too, subtly
threads its way through the interior, revealing
Tana's love affair with blue, the color of the sky
and the sea. "Think in terms of details," she
advises, "in contrast to broad brushstrokes.
That's where the magic is."

Tana speaks of the experience of living in a
small house as liberating—"allowing you to crys-
tallize the essence of what is important." Together
with the sense of neighborhood and place that
is Venice, this vintage cottage offers a model
for appropriate, sustainable living—scaled to
need, responsive to beauty, and connected to
community.

*"Serendipity played a part in where I live. It was
by chance that the house happened to go on the
market in the morning I was looking, and there it
was, in all its dilapidated glory. I had a vision of
what it could become, and others believed. Now it
is the space in which I live and work, and it is
paradise."* — Katerina Tana

Cottage Power

How does one expand and update a tumbledown beach cottage while retaining its sense of authenticity? In 1998, Barbara Baumann and Johan Feldbusch did just that with a small teardown they'd purchased on a Venice walk street.

Recent transplants from Santa Fe and the straw bale house they had built there, the couple brought with them a freewheeling sense of experimentation nurtured in the wide-open spaces of the Southwest. "Our concept was to build a beach bungalow that looked like it could have been built decades ago, but to inject it with a contemporary sense of light and openness," says Baumann, an events and public relations consultant.

ABOVE
A galvanized cattle trough, repurposed as a lily pond, becomes the centerpiece of the Jay Griffiths–designed garden. A screen of Mexican weeping bamboo offers privacy.

RIGHT
An added front deck spans the entire width of the original cottage, and announces the casual indoor-outdoor lifestyle integral to the design concept of the expanded cottage.

BELOW
Viewed through the kitchen, with
its recycled cabinetry, the back of
the house opens to a light-filled
two-story space leading to the
bedrooms upstairs.

RIGHT
The dining room offers views
of the front garden and features
a galvanized steel and iron table
by Feldbusch surrounded by
a playful mix of chairs. An old
cabinet serves as a sideboard.

It was a hands-on project. Feldbusch,
a builder-designer, gutted the cottage, leaving
three original exterior walls standing. "It looked
like a film set," declared Baumann, recalling her
years in the film business. Feldbusch poured a
foundation (there had been none), and then
built back and up. Recycled building materials
were used wherever possible—in flooring,
doors, windows, bath fixtures, and cabinets—
reflecting the couple's long-standing dedication
to both sustainability and a layered, eclectic
architectural aesthetic.

The design for the expansion emerged
from a working lunch during which the couple

sat down with friends architect Laban Wingert and designer Nancy Fishelson to explore, on the proverbial napkin, the possibilities for designing a two-story house "without a two-story feeling." Across the rear of the house, they introduced a skylit double-height space with a staircase to an open hallway on the second level, visible from below. What started as a 600-square-foot structure became, in seven short months, an 1,800-square-foot house, with access on all sides to the outdoors. At the same time, architectural detailing and inventive use of repurposed materials kept the expansion grounded in the essence of cottage.

Inside, the couple filled the house with art, furnishings—including tables made by Feldbusch—books, and collections accumulated over the years from friends, family, and travels—all personal, treasured reminders of people and experiences. The sense of openness is reinforced by the windows, left bare of coverings, thus engaging the outdoors from every room. The landscape design by Jay Griffiths reinforces the casual spirit of the house, with a pleasing balance of openness and privacy and the whimsical touch of a circular cattle-trough-cum-pond.

Baumann confesses that the cottage renovation was originally intended as a speculative venture, but the lure of Venice and the clear potential of the house soon convinced them that it was destined for them personally. Today, they look back on the effort with a great sense of fulfillment. "We feel we have completed our home and are no longer looking ahead to the next project," Baumann reflects, adding that "now is the time to enjoy it and savor what we have."

"Books, candles, artwork by friends, photographs, and travel collections make a house a home to me. I like to mix it up! Keeping the walls white and letting the color be in the artwork and collections is what I love." — Barbara Baumann

FACING PAGE
Shades of white and neutrals carry
through the cottage's interior.
Comfortable slipcovered seating
surrounds a coffee table by
Feldbusch, repurposed from a
sandblasted metal flat file cabinet.

A simple bamboo frame at the
front deck supports a reed screen
and subtly defines an outoor
seating area.

THIS PAGE
A watercolor by Elizabeth
Feldbusch and photographs by
Edward Curtis rest atop the dining
room sideboard, surrounded by a
casual arrangement of vessels of
glass. Branches of curly willow
provide an organic accent.

The master suite, vintage bathtub
and all, embodies the lighthearted,
eclectic sensibility of the cottage.
The painted open-beam ceiling is
dressed up with a simple detail to
conceal the rough roof sheathing:
narrow strips of wood set between
the rafters.

Small House, Big Heart

A small summer cottage from the 1920s nestles in the heart of a Venice neighborhood once laced with canals. Today, channeling the carefree spirit of that earlier time, two lion statues flank the front stoop, their grandiose presence offering a whimsical play on scale—and an invitation to the warmth and hospitality within.

This is a small house with a big heart. Michele Bradley, an artist, and Dick Hay, an avionics engineer, found their fixer-upper—a mere 550 square feet—in 1986. The place was in a state of total disrepair, but they immediately saw its potential. They began with the rot-

A mere 15 feet wide, its columns adorned with painted ivy, the small cottage presents a welcoming, colorful face to the neighborhood. The property also includes two small rental cottages, seen through the greenery.

ABOVE
The back deck, built by Hay, is an integral part of the cottage's living space and connects the house to Bradley's small painting studio (not shown) at the rear of the property.

Warm colors infuse the back living space, where bedroom, living area, and dining area combine. The couple has transformed a worktable into their platform bed. A potbelly stove, made in Maine and converted to gas, provides their sole source of heat. Walls are adorned with Bradley's paintings of dogs.

ted floors, and worked their way up and around the house. It was a gradual, evolving renovation, done in collaboration with a local carpenter, ensuring that the house "adapted to our lifestyle rather than us adapting to the house," Bradley says.

First, they combined a warren of small rooms at the rear of the house to make a living-dining area. They removed ceilings to lift room heights and create pockets of storage. The enclosed front porch evolved into a work space for Hay, who also built—and rebuilt—the back deck, which the couple considers an important extension of their living space. Windows are prized, essential to creating a feeling of openness and livability. And a wide hallway, connecting the front of the house to the back, reinforces that feeling of openness.

From day one, color was the key to the house. Bradley, the colorist and the painter, worked at first with a palette of clay-earth tones (still evident on the house's exterior), which has more recently given way to a play of saturated, luminous colors. Yellows, reds, and browns now infuse the cottage interior with a

The light-filled dining nook, seen from the living area, features wraparound windows softened by a simple draped fabric. Through the windows, the small rental cottages—part of the compound that also includes an art studio—are visible. The cat painting is by Bradley.

feeling of warmth and light, a change prompted in part by the loss of light when a large house was built next door.

Drawing from Hay's experience in the Navy, where he learned to appreciate small spaces, the couple approached their domestic space as though living on a boat, with everything in its place. They speak warmly and with great affection of their pleasure in inhabiting these small spaces, and how they gravitate to their small living area, enjoying each other's company, including that of their extended "family" of three dogs and two cats.

There is the community context, as well. Bradley credits the creative atmosphere of

Awash in color, the kitchen and the dining area beyond introduce rich reds into the color mix.

BELOW
The wide central hallway connects the front and back living spaces, where ceilings have been raised. A ladder accesses a storage loft above the central portion of the house, which is tightly organized, but casual in spirit.

Venice as her inspiration. "I don't think this could work anyplace else," she says. "Our house and garden can be anything that we want it to be, limited only by our imagination."

"Every area of our cottage must serve at least one purpose, either functional, aesthetic, or preferably both. We are careful not to accumulate things; actually, we seem to have more space now than when we moved in. From the beginning, we treated living in the house like living on a boat— a minimum of furniture and a lot of built-ins."
— Michele Bradley

41

The Small House Rule

The "Small House Rule" reigns at the Venice cottage of Susan and David Dworski. When anything new comes in, something must go. "When we moved here from Malibu, it felt delicious to give things away and to choose what was most meaningful," affirms Susan. Together with her husband, she oversaw a major downsizing of their residential footprint—from 4,500 square feet to a mere 1,400—at a time when they were expanding their own personal horizons of life and work.

Remarkably (and atypically for Venice), the cottage, located on one of the walk streets, was in immaculate, move-in condition when the couple bought the property in 1993, acting quickly on a lead from a real estate agent.

ABOVE
A cottage from the 1920s facing a walk street, its front portion intact, received a second-story addition in the 1970s.

RIGHT
The diminutive back garden, comprised largely of potted plants, packs plenty of green and color into a small space, creating a lush, quiet refuge.

FOLLOWING PAGES
The quiet energy of the living room at the front of the house offers an agreeable setting for evenings by the fireplace, reading, and visits with friends and neighbors.

Family photos mingle with blue and white ceramic pieces—some vintage, some discount store finds. Dancing shoes offer a whimsical reminder of good times.

LEFT
The dining area, with its casual assortment of unmatched chairs and a wall full of treasured books, shares the large space at the front of the house with the living room.

RIGHT
Floral bounty from the garden, simply arranged at the kitchen window, offers a pleasing antidote to the washing-up chores.

BOTTOM RIGHT
The open kitchen offers access to a small seating area and the living room beyond, creating a congenial flow for entertaining. A Victorian bureau mirror rests atop an antique Chinese chest and shares the wall with folk pieces collected during the couple's world travels.

LEFT
In the still of the night, the Dworskis can hear the roar of the ocean, nearly one mile away, through their master bedroom windows. In the daytime, the room is filled with light and air—a restful aerie.

BOTTOM LEFT
Antique pieces, including mirrors purchased in Italy by Susan Dworski's grandmother many years ago, bring grace and detail to the otherwise simple guest room.

FACING PAGE
The Victorian dressing table holds new and old collections, creating a play of silvers, woods, and whites.

A second-story addition from the 1970s, followed by another round of renovations by the subsequent owner, a set designer, left little for them to do. They didn't sweat the small stuff, such as the ungainly maroon bathroom tiles, realizing that their priorities resided elsewhere.

Instead, they lavished attention on creating what Susan, a designer and writer, calls their "little ecosystem, self-regulating and self-correcting." Inside, there are moments of intimacy and comfort, populated by a skillful and sometimes whimsical mix of high and low—fine family antiques, yard sale items and roadside castoffs, discount store finds, and folk art collected during years of world travel. David, a former film and television executive who now runs his own consulting firm, speaks warmly of "this snug little house" and of the simple pleasures therein, whether reading in his wingback chair by the fireplace or marveling at the late afternoon light that floods the small master bedroom upstairs. "The place is restorative," he declares.

The garden extends their living space. The lush, intimate backyard, largely a garden of potted plants, is built upon a series of decks leading to the garage, which is now a studio for Susan. The cottage-style front garden allows for interaction with the walk street neighborhood, with its steady flow of foot traffic, where "everyone knows one another—we keep an eye out for each other."

Tweak the "Small House Rule" and it becomes "Small Houses Rule." A visit to the Dworskis—showing the rewards of simplifying, that "less is more"—demonstrates just that.

"… A tiny green cottage, with sweet blooming gardens front and back. Brilliant, creative friends and neighbors. Delicious quiet day and night. No shimmering steel cars in your face. Greenery on every side. Sidewalk in front to chat up the passers-by with babies and bikes. Humane, civilized. And you can hear the Pacific Ocean roaring at 3:00 a.m. if you leave your windows open." — Susan Dworski

The Essence of Cottage

After years of searching for the perfect house, Suzanne Costello finally found it: a 1920s cottage on one of Venice's coveted walk streets, surrounded by a small garden and already renovated. The only thing missing was Costello's personal touch. "I wanted to bring out the charm, the accessibility, and the authentic feeling of a Venice beach cottage," she says.

For that reason, she rejected the idea of adding a second story, seeking to retain the original footprint and character of the 1,300-square-foot house. To create a light, airy feeling—key to the beach house sensibility she sought—she worked with designer Dayle Zukor to simplify and organize. They eliminated the bright colors from the previous renovation and replaced them with a palette of whites, creams, grayed-out blues, and greens on walls and upholstered pieces. In a move that might be viewed as counterintuitive, they darkened the wood floors, using them to anchor the small rooms and allow furniture, rugs, and accessories to pop.

A few key pieces chosen early in the design process—a vintage Chinese farm table, a custom green-leather desk chair, and a fabric for the sofa—informed the rest of the interior selections. Small moves, such as topping inexpensive lamp bases with custom lampshades, lend the house its distinctive designer air. Costello fondly refers to this strategy, one of the designer's favorites, as "a delicious splurge, what we called 'Dayle-ing it up.'"

Banks of roses define the front garden of this 1920s walk-street cottage, its color echoing the blooms of the jacaranda tree.

LEFT
The original dining room has been transformed into a TV viewing area. Beyond, the new kitchen-dining addition is visible.

RIGHT
Custom swiveling upholstered armchairs in the front sitting room surround a storage basket that doubles as a coffee table. An antique Biedermeier cabinet occupies the "gift-wrapping" nook beyond.

BOTTOM RIGHT
The new kitchen-dining area, with its open-beam ceilings, skylights, and fireplace, steps down from the floor level at the front of the house, permitting easy access to the rear outdoor decks.

At the heart of the cottage's renovated floor plan is a generously sized kitchen-dining area, which sets the tone for the easygoing flow of the house. Well-thought-out furniture groupings reinforce the cottage's open, inviting atmosphere, while two small bedrooms offer a sense of quiet intimacy. Outside, the house is surrounded by a series of small outdoor decks and spaces, each with its own character, and the front yard, with its lush plantings of roses and flowering plants, signals "cottage" the moment it is glimpsed.

Costello, a real estate agent by trade, understands the ingredients of a desirable property, but when it came to her own house, she was taken aback by the power of the experience. "I love my home," she declares, adding, "I never knew that a house could give you so much happiness." It's a pleasure that's shared with members of the community each time they walk by.

"When I began the search for my home, I had a long list of the things I felt I needed. In exploring Venice, it was apparent that compromises were going to be necessary. After a year in the house, I realized that I'd rather have half of what I need here than one hundred percent anywhere else."
— Suzanne Costello

Good Vibrations

I f "a little help from my friends" was ever an apt motif for a home renovation project, then this 1920s Colonial cottage, nestled in a vintage courtyard, would qualify. The house belongs to Renée Montagne, public radio journalist, who moved here in 1993 as a renter. She fell in love with the place and, several years later, was able to buy her cottage—all 1,000 square feet of it.

But there was work to be done, and Montagne moved forward with characteristic energy and verve, enlisting the ideas and expertise of friends who shared her enthusiasm for the house. "This was a collaborative, on-site, evolving process," she recalls. "We improvised solutions as we went."

LEFT
Reflecting the setting sun, the pedimented porch of this Colonial cottage—one of five in a 1920s-era courtyard—suggests a step back in time.

ABOVE
An outdoor dining pergola occupies the space of a former dog run, transformed with the help of designer-builders Lorri and Bob Ramirez, who also designed the signature tile wall feature.

57

LEFT
A view of the kitchen from the dining area shows custom cherry cabinets by Mark Feinberg, a friend of the owner. The new pair of French doors offers the all-important connection to the outdoor living area at the rear.

BELOW
Montagne's self-described "passion for pottery" is apparent in this collection from France and Afghanistan, purchased during travels and while on assignment. The covered wooden dish and beaded bowl are from South Africa.

A previous remodel had dramatically reconfigured the space in the front of the house, lifting the ceiling and combining rooms. Building on this, Montagne proceeded to maximize the potential that the rest of cottage offered. With the help of designer-builders Lorri and Bob Ramirez, she added new doors and windows that opened the house to small outdoor patios, bringing in light and air and creating new vistas. Bathrooms were updated, and flooring

ABOVE
The front portion of the cottage—the living and dining area—features high ceilings and an open floor plan, creating a feeling of spaciousness. Visible beyond are small rooms—bedrooms, baths, and study, in nearly their original configuration. The remodeled kitchen is partially visible to the right.

FACING PAGE, TOP
The master bedroom, with a view to an outdoor tiled shower, features luxuriant light-blocking window coverings that accommodate the sleep schedule of the owner, whose workday often begins in the wee-small-hours of the morning.

FACING PAGE, BOTTOM
The cottage window and door in the small guest bedroom were added for air circulation and access to the outdoors. Decorative items include a mirror from Montagne's antique mirror collection, early-nineteenth-century French prints, and beaded African stools.

renewed. The work proceeded quickly, as though on a journalist's deadline, and the entire remodel was accomplished in four short months.

Inside, Montagne furnished the cottage in a spirit of international eclecticism, reflecting her years of travel and work abroad. Collections of pottery from such far-flung locations as Afghanistan, Africa, and France grace shelving and tables, while a diverse collection of mirrors and antique prints adorn the walls.

There are also the especially treasured objects, each with a story. A prime example: a simple wooden desk chair, bought in South Africa at a secondhand store, that Montagne used when she was on assignment reporting on the release of Nelson Mandela. "It took some doing to get the chair back to the States," she recalls, "but it was worth all of the effort."

Montagne also put considerable effort into the shared courtyard. Working with her neighbors, she spearheaded the transformation of the common areas, taking up the old concrete slabs and breaking them into pavers laced with ground cover—a surface suitable for both cars and people—and renewing the landscape with trees, shrubs, and color. Her goal: to bring back the spirit of the courtyard—all five cottages and garages—as it was in the 1920s.

Stepping through the front gate into the courtyard today might seem like a step back in time. Yet a closer look reveals this to be a place very much in the here and now, celebrating collaboration and friendship, and engaged in the broader world.

"I came to L.A. with very little in the way of furnishings, but with many small treasures carried back from my life in South Africa and my childhood in the South Pacific. I think of my cottage as a lovely wooden boat, carrying my life forward, festooned with bright bits of everywhere I've been, and everything I've seen and done."
— Renée Montagne

Canal Living

The vista along one of the six
remaining Venice canals captures
the romance of this place out of
time. In recent decades, new, large
lot-filling homes have replaced the
intimate cottages of Venice's early
years. Still, the magic persists.

A Passion for Old Things

Take a dollop of New England country, add a generous dash of the bohemian, casual spirit of Venice, mix it together with the theatrical flair of the owners, and you have the home of Orson Bean and Alley Mills on the Venice canals. Among the last of a rapidly disappearing species—the original canal cottages—three adjacent houses, two of them connected, form a lively family compound.

"Our doors and windows are always open," declares Bean, who, with his wife and fellow actor Mills, sets the tone for a free-flow of energy, movement, and hospitality in, out, and around their compound. They admit to spending almost as much time outdoors as in,

A trio of cottages forms the family's compound, balancing privacy and community. The expansive front deck of the main cottage, at the center, is used almost daily by the owners. It embodies the welcoming, inclusive spirit of Venice.

ABOVE
A casual, lively arrangement of photos and memorabilia celebrates family and work.

RIGHT
The single great room of the main cottage is where family life happens—cooking, dining, and socializing. Visible overhead are tensioned cables stretched across the full width and length of the cottage, tying the perimeter walls together. Visible to the right is the sun-filled passageway connecting to the cottage next door, the owners' private retreat.

whether on the expansive deck overlooking the canals, or in the comfortably landscaped backyard that runs the length of the three houses, and where several generations of the Bean–Mills family often gather.

The main cottage, built in 1912, forms the heart of the compound. Bean opened up the 800-square-foot structure in the 1990s, remov-ing rafters, installing turnbuckles that tie perimeter walls together, and rebuilding floors with thick planks to create a great room. This is where life happens—eating, cooking, visiting, making music. Next door, connected to the main cottage through a corridor bridge, is the couple's private retreat—a vine-covered Span-ish stucco cottage with a second-story addi-

FACING PAGE
Weathered garden furniture—wicker and wood—offers casual seating in the great room, where the rule is: no upholstered furniture. Architectural paintings are by James Michalopoulos. The portrait of Bean is by Michael Alatza.

RIGHT
Connected to the main cottage is the vine-covered stucco bungalow that serves as the couple's private retreat and sleeping quarters, with its rustic fireplace, textured walls, and saltillo tile floors.

BOTTOM RIGHT
Adjacent to the windows overlooking the backyard is the rustic dining table, the mirror at its end playfully expanding the sense of space.

tion. Flanking the other side of the main cottage is another vintage bungalow used as a guest house, its original features intact.

With Mills' passion for Americana, history, and "old things," ("including me," Bean quips), she has populated the spaces with "stuff we love." Both she and Bean have roots in rural New England—New Hampshire and Vermont, respectively—and she recalls weekends as a child scouting antiques in old barns with her mother, an art editor at *American Heritage*.

She continues to collect. Gathering family antiques and memorabilia, art and artifacts—all connected through family, friends, and local vintage shops—she has orchestrated lively, relaxed, and eclectic groupings of furniture and objects while observing her cardinal rule: no upholstered furniture.

Speaking of cardinal, Mills is devoted to things red—the "color of life, of warmth, and passion." Red accents punctuate the principal living spaces of the compound, inside and out, signaling the couple's lively, generous engagement with life, work, family, and friends. This spirit extends to the community outside. Says Mills, "I love living on the canals—we invite passers-by to visit, have a glass of wine, and share the beauty and spirit of this wonderful place."

"We've gone sideways and tied three little joints together, so we have room to live in plus a big yard. Before long, we're afraid we'll have the only original cottages left on the canals. Venice is unique. It was founded back in 1905 for amusement, not commerce, as most communities are. It had roller coasters and camel rides and the old spirit of fun still lives on." — Orson Bean

The lively, eclectic mix of furniture and found objects brings a sense of the outdoors in, and includes a porch swing from Maine, a boat retrieved from an amusement park ride, and a painted Moroccan tabouret.

Boho Chic

I f there ever were a house that channeled, and then updated, the rustic bohème spirit of the Venice of decades past, this would be the place. When the screenwriting duo Geoffrey and Marcia Blake bought their canal-facing bungalow in 1995, the former hippie-pad was in a complete state of disrepair. Abandoned and in foreclosure, it was known to locals as the "Judy Collins house" for the 1970s-era mural painted across its façade.

The bungalow had somehow survived the first big wave of demolitions along the Venice canals that began in the 1980s, as early-twentieth-century summer cottages made way for outsized, lot-filling stucco boxes. Yet this one—

Despite renovations over the years, this canal-side house, with its mature trees and generous front deck, retains its vintage, casual feel. The family maintains a dock and small rowboat, always at the ready, for canal excursions.

73

The living room embodies the spirit of multicultural harmony, with furniture, accessories, and art sourced from around the world. Sumatran masks purchased during travels in Bali are reflected in the mirror.

built in 1910 in nearby Ocean Park and moved to the site in 1915—had already been enlarged with a setback second story, and was thus a prime candidate for renewal by a sympathetic steward.

The Blakes were a perfect fit. "Our goal was to bring the house back," says Geoffrey, who also works as an actor, describing their approach to the renovation, much of which he did himself. The couple sought to retain the woodsy, vintage feel of the original while making some concessions to modernity. These included a new heating system in place of the single fireplace that had been the home's sole source of heat; an energy-conserving tankless water heater; and a skylight, bought at a local swap meet, to brighten the dark bungalow interior.

The patina of age and history carries inside, but with a twist. Marcia describes the approach as "indigenous coffee bar chic"—a skillfully orchestrated collection of furniture, rugs, art, and accessories sourced from around the world, some from their travels, the rest acquired locally. The spirit is one of multicultural harmony in which pieces from Bali, Mexico, Jamaica, India, Afghanistan, and the American Southwest mix it up in a play of rich earth colors and textures. Drums from the Taos pueblo that once served as side tables have now been returned to their original function—as rhythm instruments for the Blakes' young son.

Life at the Blake bungalow is also lived outdoors. They enjoy the canals on their small pad-

LEFT
The dining room features a vintage table and benches purchased from a church in Mexico, a chandelier converted to candle power and found at a local thrift store, and a 1930s stained glass window, a swap meet discovery.

RIGHT
Upstairs, the master bedroom has access to the roof deck, which offers both canal views and a sense of privacy.

dleboat, the *Blaketanic*. The expansive front deck—one of three outdoor living areas—extends its invitation to all passers-by, and with its carved wooden signs, unapologetically wears its heart on its sleeve. Marcia explains, "We call our house 'the love shack.' It's here that we feel immense gratitude for our life together as a family—a wonderful, peaceful place to write and work and be with one another."

"Our front deck is great for sightseeing. So many people stroll on the canals, and in the summer, all the neighbors are out and socializing—which is wonderful." — Geoffrey Blake

LEFT
The child's room, at the rear of the house, has access to the back deck.

ABOVE
At the front of the house, the small office, with its whitewashed slat walls, mixes the modern and the vintage. Sudanese tribal pieces flank a framed drawing by Giora.

Bungalow Spirit

This row of original Venice
"vacation villas" occupies a wedge-
shaped block known as The Island,
at one time surrounded entirely by
canals. In 1929, after years of civic
controversy, most of the canals
were filled and replaced by ever-
so-modern roadways.

Channeling Arts & Crafts

A successful renovation is one that captures the essence—the inner voice—of a house. When Sue Kaplan bought her small Craftsman bungalow on a Venice walk street in 1998, the house had been painted white inside and out, its original character obscured by a previous owner's image of a beach cottage.

This was the logical place to start. "I wanted to get the woodwork back," recalls Kaplan of the arduous task of stripping wood of its layers of paint. "Once the wood expressed itself, the house became the Venice bungalow of its origins—a workingman's bungalow—true to the neighborhood." Similarly, she transformed the

One of the first houses to be built in this neighborhood of walk streets, this early-twentieth-century Craftsman home displays the characteristic low-gabled roof of the classic California bungalow. The deeply inset front porch serves as an outdoor room. Chair cushions feature an Arts & Crafts–inspired floral motif.

house's exterior, removing the asbestos siding to find the bungalow's original wood siding, a special bonus.

The work advanced in stages, beginning with the thoroughly modern Craftsman kitchen. "Then I sat on it," says Kaplan, referring to the five-year hiatus she took from renovation work while she lived in the house, wanting to experience it on a deeper level before making a commitment to the next round of work.

As a historian of the book and a letterpress printer, Kaplan has a keen sense of what it means to immerse oneself in the spirit of a time. Thus, research into the Arts & Crafts movement became a focus of this incubation period. "I have always been more entranced by the past than the present," she admits. With that inclination, she turned her attention again to the house, selecting colors, restoring the fireplace, and—with the help of interior designer Dayle Zukor—furnishing the rooms with both

ABOVE
A Gustav Stickley sideboard fills the space once occupied by the bungalow's original built-in buffet.

RIGHT
Authentic Arts & Crafts pieces mix gracefully with new custom pieces, including Greene & Greene-inspired living room chairs by Venice woodworker Stephen Ritson. Paint colors are drawn from period fabrics and rugs, and the glow from a vintage Handel art glass chandelier fills the dining room. Paintings are by Conrad Buff and, over the sideboard, Leonard Baskin.

signature vintage and custom pieces, the latter fabricated by local artisans.

Throughout the house, there are places of repose—cozy spots for reading and basking in the pleasure of the surroundings. Kaplan's favorite spot is the small sunroom at the front of the house. Likely a former sleeping porch, it is small, compact, and filled with light; the original windows, with their rolled, wavy glass, offer a pleasing vista into the front garden. "Even the cats love this room," says Kaplan.

Like so many California bungalows, the house has an easy relationship to the outdoors. The expansive front porch is almost a room unto itself, and two private side gardens, each with its own character, augment the possibilities for indoor-outdoor living.

"I have tried to interpret the Arts & Crafts spirit for today," Kaplan says, adding, "The house had a voice, and I wanted to honor that, while at the same time making it work for a contemporary lifestyle." With Kaplan's careful, purposeful renovation, it is clear that she has done just that.

"I needed to make this a purposeful house. My rooms are small. Every space counts, and furnishings must be chosen with care. I have public rooms and private rooms, a public garden and a private, more contemplative one. As the gardens seem to draw you into the house, and the house's vistas pull you outside, so do people move in and out and settle in and enjoy themselves."
— Sue Kaplan

FACING PAGE, TOP LEFT
The living room fireplace, with its mantelshelf, flanking cabinets, and casement windows meticulously returned to their original finish, is faced in reproduction Batchelder tiles.

FACING PAGE, BOTTOM LEFT
The guest room also serves as a quiet retreat, its sofa upholstered in a fabric designed by William Morris.

FACING PAGE, RIGHT
Handmade tiles complement the zigzag patterns of the gas cooktop in Kaplan's thoroughly modern Craftsman kitchen.

ABOVE
The sunroom overlooks the front garden. The original sliding windows retain their vintage rolled glass, its wavy imperfections lending extra character to the space.

Space
Continuum

Still evolving, the century-old house of Sherie and Mel Scheer is an authentic Venice original. Located on a walk street developed by Abbot Kinney himself, the house began life as an unpretentious two-story beach bungalow, and today offers a vision of contemporary sophistication, tempered by the desire for simplicity.

When the couple bought the house in 1975, the bungalow showed the grit of age and circumstance, with a small rear addition from the 1940s that had converted the house into a duplex. Still, there was no question that it was a keeper, its basic architectural character intact—needing work, but with enormous potential.

So with this, the Scheers embarked on a project more than three decades long—one that continues to this day—offering an inspiring case study of the evolution of a house as it parallels the lives of its inhabitants.

A back room, for example, has seen several incarnations, serving variously as an art studio, their daughter's bedroom, a guest room, and most recently modernized as a TV–reading room—the best "nap place in the whole house, and my favorite spot for reading," says Sherie. Similarly, the enclosed front porch, which began as a playroom, later became a bedroom, then a guest room, now serves as a small home office and reading nook, a spot favored by Mel, a physician.

FACING PAGE
The distinctive
telescoped dormer
lends character to
the shingled and
clapboard façade
of this original Venice
beach bungalow, built
in 1907 on a narrow
30-foot lot. The
original double-hung
windows were
replaced with
casements during
a 1980s remodel.

RIGHT
A screen of flowering
plums defines the
edge of the small back
deck, simply adorned
with a patterned
outdoor rug and
a border of potted
cymbidiums. The
rebuilt garage and the
stairs leading to the
yoga studio above are
visible through the
trees.

Sherie's imprint on the house is every-where. An artist and yoga practitioner, she has brought to this lifelong project a disciplined design sensibility that the self-described farm girl from Iowa calls "subtle but cheerful." Add to this her studies in ikebana, and you have an aesthetic that translates to a rich but disciplined domestic environment with a careful orchestration of color, form, and space.

"I am constantly editing and paring," says Sherie, "in my search for simplicity." Clutter is anathema, but she is deeply devoted to her favorite things—whether a Noguchi table, a Navajo rug, her California pottery, or her collection of art and ethnic crafts, acquired from friends or through travels. The inspiration carries over to the outdoors. The small, well-structured garden avoids the starkness of minimalism, yet simplicity rules.

So it is that this home from another era, with its easy flow of space and its distinctive Craftsman aura, has proven remarkably adaptable to the Scheers' contemporary lifestyle. This bungalow's story is one of both continuity and change, but at its core, it continues to celebrate the essential values of simplicity, balance, and discipline, carrying the spirit of the Arts & Crafts into the twenty-first century.

"Through several remodels, we have never hesitated to integrate the contemporary approach of continuous, flowing space. We regard our home as pliable; since we moved in, we have continually honed it to our tastes and uses, often changing the way rooms are used. It is simple, uncluttered, and comfortable. We plan to continue living here in our old age." — Sherie Scheer

FACING PAGE
The original front porch, now enclosed, spans the full width of the house, and is one of the owners' favorite spaces. Surrounded on three sides by greenery and light, it comprises three zones: the entryway, a small office, and a reading nook. Surfboard art by Gilbert "Magú" Luján.

ABOVE
The living room, with the enclosed front porch visible beyond, features original woodwork—wainscoting and ceiling beams—painted for a light, contemporary look. The custom-mixed white, developed by Sherie Scheer, contains quiet undertones of yellow and gold ochre.

LEFT
Continuing the process of renovation and renewal, the back room, now a TV and reading room, connects to the back deck through a pair of French doors. Ikebana-inspired flower arrangements throughout the house are by the owner. Watercolor by Keisho Okayama.

BOTTOM LEFT
Textiles from Indonesia and Indian fabric draperies offer an air of soft relaxation in the master bedroom. Paintings by Robert Burtis.

RIGHT
The flow of space between the principal living areas is evident in this view from the dining room, through the living room, and into the front porch. To create a visual connection between the kitchen and the dining area, the owners removed a wall at counter height (to the left, not visible in the photo), adding to the sense of openness. Collage by Richard Turner.

Venice rooftops and the blue Pacific beyond are visible from the roof deck, which sits atop a two-story garage-studio at the rear of the property, built in 1988.

Pushing the Envelope, Gently

Their modest 1908 Craftsman beach bungalow—no matter how beloved— just wasn't working for Jacky Lavin and Brian Finney. They needed more space, and selling wasn't an attractive option. Such a move would almost certainly have doomed this vintage dwelling to the wrecking ball, a prospect that simply went against the grain.

So they approached architect Tom Egidi of Tuna Studio, asking for an addition that would offer a modern equivalent of Craftsman while retaining the character of the original house, with its authentic, handmade charm. Although the small urban lot dictated building up, says Finney, "we sought to situate the addition sufficiently far back to keep it out of sight for anyone walking past it."

LEFT
The small Craftsman bungalow retains it vintage charm—rafter tails, dormer, brackets, and all— while sporting a compatible second-floor addition, visible at the rear. Gate and fence design by Tom Egidi of Tuna Studio.

ABOVE
The tranquil shade garden at the front of the house, designed by Ann Meshekoff of Ground Effects, utilizes mortarless pavers and ground cover to create a sense of a meandering natural space.

LEFT
The passion for color plays throughout the house. In the living room, apple green walls and painted woodwork offer a foil for the couple's collections of pottery and carnival ware. Throughout the house, floral arrangements by Jacky Lavin complement their surroundings.

BELOW
A piece of neon art by Lavin occupies a prominent spot in the entry porch. Resting on top are two pieces from her collection of antlers, treasured for their form and tactile qualities.

FOLLOWING PAGES
A close-up view of the couple's collection of vintage American and European animal creamers reveals a play of forms and colors. This collection, along with others throughout the house, demonstrates the passionate collector's mantra of "more is more."

BELOW
The new kitchen at the rear of the house carries forward the color palette of greens and yellows, with a durable linoleum floor underfoot and backsplash tiles from a local craftsman.

RIGHT
In the former dining room, now a media room, the ceiling opening brings light to the center of the house. A small shrine cabinet, visible through the passageway that leads to the kitchen, contains collections of small objects, including artifacts discovered during excavations around the house.

Egidi devised an inventive solution, opening the house in the middle with a staircase to the setback second-story master suite, and, further up, to the exclamation point of a small glass-roofed retreat—the "moon room"—that opens to the outdoors. The added bonus: a cascade of natural light, plus passive ventilation that cools the entire house.

ABOVE
Upstairs, a vintage microscope
cabinet rescued during a remodel
at a nearby university serves to
both define the office space and
create separation from the
adjacent master bedroom.

FACING PAGE
The upstairs addition culminates
in the rooftop "moon room,"
where light from the glazed roof
pours into the spaces below.
Abstract mobile by Melvin
Detroit.

"We tried to be inventive with our remodel," says Lavin, a floral designer and artist, "but we also treasured the house's history." In this spirit, they were rewarded during the excavation for a new foundation, discovering artifacts discarded long ago—a small china doll and a metal printing plate, among other items—now displayed lovingly in a special "shrine" that could easily be mistaken for a cabinet of curiosities. Using the original brick, the couple oversaw the careful rebuilding of the fireplace and previously unreinforced chimney. In another nod to period detail, vintage or salvaged fixtures were used throughout.

Inside, the house gracefully showcases the couple's collections against a backdrop of carefully orchestrated color, Lavin's passion. Whether in the display of carnival glass, Mexican crafts, or fine art photography, a sense of discovery and delight awaits. And as for the inevitable space issues: "You can always find room for something else," says Lavin. "You just need to be inventive about storage and display."

Finney, a professor of English literature, speaks warmly about the evolution of their bungalow and neighborhood over two decades. "We love living in Venice, with its diverse, friendly population, and its many cottages and houses that jostle so close to one another," he says. Their small front garden, embodying a rustic cottage spirit, is an apt illustration of this sense of community, with its cascading 80-year-old rose vine, growing, in fact, over the picket fence from the yard next door.

"We wanted a contemporary design for the added structure which echoed but did not imitate the 1908 original building. We knew that we could have added far more space had we demolished and rebuilt a maxed-out house, but we have no regrets for what we chose to do. We hope that, by remodeling, we have ensured a long life for the original cottage that, with its odd nooks and eccentric architectural features, gives us so much pleasure." — Brian Finney

IMAGINATION

Evolving over Time

" This house is a temple engaged in the celebration of life." A credo, carved on a piece of reclaimed wood, announces the purpose and the spirit of a remarkable expanded bungalow, situated on an idiosyncratic five-sided lot at the angled intersection of two streets, formerly canals, in the heart of the historic Venice.

When Tim and Robin Rudnick found their home in 1972, they began as renters of the original small California bungalow, 800 square feet in total. A threatened eviction one year later turned into an opportunity to buy. And, to

LEFT
The new wing connects to the vintage bungalow, just visible through the tree, and wraps around a large garden area that resembles a natural landscape with a California wetlands feel.

ABOVE
The music room comprises one of the three zones of the house—"art, community, and hearth." Light pours in from a recycled storefront window.

The original bungalow serves as the "hearth" of the house—intimate and warm. It connects to the new wing and the dining area to the right. The garden is visible through the casement windows flanking the fireplace. A Moroccan rug, one of several in the house, provides a warm jolt of color and pattern.

their surprise, their purchase encompassed a previously fenced-off corner portion of the property (assumed incorrectly to be separate), providing them with an opportunity to shape a remarkable domestic compound.

With a young family and budget constraints, it took a bit of time to begin—15 years, to be exact—yet the gestation period was put to good use. "We had plenty of time to plan and develop the concept for the house," says Tim, a conservationist and ocean activist. "We decided we were going to live in a house of light."

Robin, a public school teacher and arts administrator, offered steady guidance as Tim first visualized, then designed. The driving idea behind the expansion involved changing the orientation of the house, shifting the focus to the corner yard and creating a new line of access with the addition of a pavilion-like wing (a pagoda, Tim calls it) that wraps around the yard, breaking the rectilinear axis to frame the view of the garden. "Like arms," says Tim, "the shape of the house embraces the outside."

At the heart of the house is the kitchen-dining area that occupies the midpoint of the angled floor plan. It serves as a point of connection between the old bungalow and the new wing, which also contains a music room and upstairs bedrooms.

The community space at the
center of the house, where the
new wing joins the old, radiates a
casual, welcoming spirit. The
angled configuration opens the
interior to the light and the view
of the garden outside. The
dishwasher-free kitchen, inspired
by a photo of an Italian kitchen
in an old *Time-Life* cookbook,
features a capacious marble sink,
a commercial range, and a pot
rack rescued from a local
restaurant. The lithograph is by
Ruth Weisberg.

Collections of African baskets
and California pottery,
including a grouping of vintage
green Bauer bowls, occupy
surfaces at every level, and mix
comfortably with tableware
and other utilitarian objects.

Integral to both the lively aesthetic and the
environmental ethic of the house are the
repurposed and recycled parts, fixtures and
materials—an old church banister, a window
from an old restaurant, skylights, and bathroom
sinks, to name a few. A sophisticated yet informal mix of furnishings, art, and decorative
pieces represents several decades' worth of
acquisitions from yard sales, local shops, and
family collections.

The house continues to evolve. "I'd be sorry
if it were ever finished," says Robin. Adds Tim: "I
object to the notion of a house as a 'machine
for living.' Instead, it should celebrate the act of
living." This premise inspires the Rudnicks in the
creative process that continues to shape their
house—as a place for family, for friends, and
for the simple pleasures of daily life.

*"There is a constant dialogue in our home
between old and new. We sought to maintain
both sensibilities—valuing the dark, intimate
spaces of the old bungalow, and celebrating
the new—which is all about light and space."*
— Tim Rudnick

113

ABOVE
A garden aesthetic defines a charming yet functional bathroom. A wrought iron pot stand is recycled to hold a sink basin, found in Mexico, and faucets, garden style, project from the wall.

RIGHT
The second floor of the new wing includes the master bedroom, with its play of natural wood tones, organic textures, white walls, and light. A Guatemalan textile covers the bed, and beaded necklaces, artfully hung on a branch and along a recycled window, provide a decorative accent.

Contemporary Cool

Surfers enjoy another
glorious day under the sun,
with the expanse of Venice
Beach, the boardwalk, and
the neighborhoods beyond,
stretching before them.

Bungalow at the Edge

Their small California bungalow, when built in 1924, fronted on one of the original (and now filled-in) Venice canals. Today, while referencing a time past, the home of Douglas Speidel and Robert Greene exudes a hip, contemporary vibe, with a stylish dose of retro that leaves no question as to the century you are in and the culture you are celebrating: sophisticated, urban, and global.

When they bought the house in 1999, Greene and Speidel found a recently renovated bungalow—modernized inside by the previous owners (architects Susan Addison and Jeffrey Sherbeck), with an intact, vintage exterior and a

LEFT
Mid-Century Modern meets California Bungalow with an updated roof profile, a slatted fence, and structured plantings. Front windows remain unobstructed, maintaining a visual connection between the house and the surrounding neighborhood.

ABOVE
A vignette from the garden patio portrays a decidedly modern vibe.

RIGHT
An open floor plan with
strategically placed partition
walls creates a lively series of
connected spaces at the front
of the house. One of Robert
Greene's paintings serves as a
focal point for the room, with
its carefully edited collection
of classic modernist pieces,
most purchased at local shops.

FOLLOWING PAGES
The guest room, built in a
converted garage, displays an
abstract by Greene, and above
the daybed, a printed textile
panel.

small bedroom/bath addition at the rear.
"We kept the essence of what we were given,"
says Speidel, a creative director of an advertising agency," and then made it work."

What they were given was a tightly orchestrated series of spaces, featuring a play of cubic
volumes that both define rooms and ingen-
iously accommodate storage. Adding to the
spatial interest are ceiling heights that vary by
room. All of this is contained within a bungalow
with an exceedingly small footprint—only 700
square feet.

Inside, they started by painting all of the
walls white, and then began to populate the
rooms with a rich and provocative mix of signature contemporary and vintage pieces, many
purchased locally at nearby shops and galleries.
"My decorative inspiration is Italian Modernism
from the '60s and '70s," says Greene, an artist
whose paintings grace the walls alongside thrift-
shop finds and works by friends and colleagues.
The result is a disciplined tapestry of fanciful,
individual sensibilities.

Outside, they started from scratch. After
working with landscape architects Jay Griffiths
and Russ Cletta to structure the spaces, Speidel

RIGHT
A partition doubling as a storage unit defines one edge of the main living area. Beyond, a wall of drawers in the master bedroom is visible. To the right, doors to the outdoors extend the living space to the decks, constructed at the same level as the wide-plank maple floors to create a continuous surface.

FOLLOWING PAGES
Every square inch of the small urban lot has been used to maximize outdoor living space. Douglas Speidel designed and built all of the outdoor decks and installed the landscaping according to a layout designed by Jay Griffiths and Russ Cletta.

planted and detailed every square inch on the tight urban lot to create "wall-to-wall plants"— a thoroughgoing labor of love. He also designed and built the decks that surround the house, as well as the front fence that serves as the new entry. And while privacy is always at a premium in Venice, Speidel is quick to point out that this fence stops at the bungalow's front windows, thus maintaining the house's visual connection with the neighborhood.

"Ours is a synergistic do-it-yourself collaboration," says Speidel of the house, "combining Robert's artistic vision with my pragmatic, hands-on, getting-it-done approach." While acknowledging the bungalow's quintessential California features, Greene—who hails from New York City—describes their dwelling as "a kind of New York apartment, what we call a 'floor-through,' because when you step outside, you're in the city." This time, the city is Venice, a place that embodies everything they value about urban living.

"It was important to us that our bungalow retain the integrity of its 'cottage scale' and vintage architectural character at the street front. The modern volumes and sensibility emerge as one moves through the house." — Robert Greene

Laboratory for Small and Big Ideas

"It is an architect's dream, to work on one's own house," says Steven Shortridge of the small stucco bungalow he has been shaping for more than a decade. The 750-square-foot house, wedged on a tight corner lot, is a fragment of a larger Spanish–Mediterranean house, and was moved to the site in the 1930s. Having been abandoned for eight years prior to Shortridge buying it in 1996, the house may have seemed an unlikely candidate for renewal by an architect known for his modernist aesthetic, but he was challenged by the opportunity to use it as a kind of sounding board—a laboratory for both small and big ideas.

LEFT
Approached through a garden of subdued greens, the house, with its luminous ochre walls, offers a jolt of color, and the entry canopy suggests rays of sunshine.

ABOVE
The dining nook behind the louvered screen features a pendant lamp by Alison Berger.

From the compact living room with its classic modernist pieces, the kitchen can be glimpsed through the opening above the vintage built-in sideboard. Thick exterior walls, visible through the windows at the left, create opportunities to accommodate indirect lighting, thus accentuating the sculpted space.

The changes evolved incrementally, over time. "Once I moved in, I was able to experience the house and think through all of the opportunities," says Shortridge. As an opening salvo, he shifted the entry to the rear of the house, with access from the alley at the side of the fenced property. This reorientation had the benefit of activating the alley, an often underutilized resource, encouraging its use as a pedestrian passage to the shops and restaurants of the nearby Abbot Kinney Boulevard.

Inside the gated entry, a private, lushly landscaped outdoor living area, designed with the help of Jay Griffiths, leads to the new "front door" of the house, surrounded by a smart composition of wood, metal and glass, including a canopy and bank of louvers that offer shade from the strong western sun.

Within the house, every inch matters. Shortridge focused on spatial continuity and sight lines in a tightly orchestrated sequence of rooms. Varied ceiling heights, built-in cabinets and furniture, indirect lighting, and bold colors work together to define spaces in often surprising ways, and offer interest into what would be considered small rooms by any standard. Playful touches, such as a high window in the bedroom or a small skylight that straddles both kitchen and bathroom, add wit to this inventive and highly disciplined interior.

The house also encourages dialogue between old and new, and allows for a certain degree of ambiguity and a sense of layering. Original windows coexist comfortably with

Viewed from the living room, the
study–master suite area occupies the street-
facing portion (and former front) of the
house. Original casings and moldings have
been retained, along with the jalousie
windows from an earlier remodel, now
acceptable in their hybrid context of old and
new. Paintings (left to right) are by Darren
Waterson and Sam Messer.

Custom casework of vertical grain
Douglas fir mixed with stained MDF
panels integrates shelving, storage,
and work surfaces. The unit also
serves to divide the work area from
the compact bedroom, its sense of
space enhanced by a raised ceiling
and high window.

LEFT
The kitchen offers a refined integration of old and new. Sleek new cabinetry floats off the linoleum flooring, meeting original millwork and windows unapologetically, but respectfully.

ABOVE
Contemporary Swedish glass enlivens the relocated sideboard, and references color from the kitchen beyond.

135

new jalousie windows. Period moldings are juxtaposed with contemporary woodwork and detailing. The old oak floors, with their imperfections and stains, continue to serve honorably. Shortridge emphasizes the original volume of the house, with its 14-inch-thick exterior walls, through the application of a smooth stucco finish to the outside. "The house," he says, "now looks as though it were cut from a single piece of clay."

In a very real sense, Shortridge has not only renewed a modest house, but has transformed it, thanks to the luxury of time and the willingness to imagine. Thus, a small house with big ideas demonstrates—in no uncertain terms— that size is what you make of it.

"My approach to the design of my house is to consider every inch of space as important—inside and out, and even the borrowed landscape outside of the property boundaries. This approach has given the house a feeling of size much larger than the actual numbers would seem to indicate."
— Steven Shortridge

ABOVE
Shortridge has landscaped the alley running along the side of the property as part of the larger move of reorienting the entry sequence from the front to the back of the house. The added benefit is the activation and enhancement of the alley as a valued urban space.

RIGHT
A steel plate wall and a perimeter of bamboo define the boundaries of the house's new front yard and create an outdoor room, with generous banquettes and fire pit accent.

A Beach Cottage, Transformed

An original Venice beach cottage, a stone's throw from the boardwalk, embodies in microcosm the evolving history of Venice. Built as a weekend cottage in 1906, only a year after the founding of Venice, today it is a sophisticated dwelling for a professional couple—Linda Lucks, a nonprofit consultant and community activist, and Michael Rosenthal, an attorney.

"When I bought the house in 1973, as a single mom, it was a great place to raise my two children," she recalls, adding, "I knew I wanted to live here for my entire life." It was a formative time for the community: Venice was being discovered by young families seeking an alternative to L.A. suburban neighborhoods, and a feeling of adventure and experimentation was in the air. Evidence of the house's past—as a boardinghouse complete with pot-bellied stoves in each bedroom—was discernible, and when Lucks bought the house, it had been converted to a duplex.

Years later, with children grown, Lucks—now in a new chapter of her life with Michael—decided it was time for a major remodel to bring her beach cottage into the twenty-first century. With the help of architect Peter Choate, an old friend, Lucks oversaw a total remodel of the house, reorganizing the space and opening walls as much as possible. The original cluster of kitchen, bedroom and

The simple forms of this original Venice
house are apparent, even after a century
of change—the gabled, pedimented
roof and trios of double-hung windows.
A smooth-stucco finish offers a
contemporary, updated air. The front porch,
once open to the garden, is now enclosed
to accommodate an expanded living room
area and bring more light inside.

LEFT
The living room offers a serene, contemporary update of a beach cottage, along with a mix of Asian pieces—cloisonné, ceramics, and chests—collected over the years.

BELOW
A view to the front garden, originally laid out by landscape designer Jay Griffiths. The house fronts on one of Venice's original walk streets, adjacent to the boardwalk.

ABOVE
At the rear of the house, the new kitchen displays collections of pottery and seltzer bottles grouped by color. An antique chandelier hangs over the dining table, surrounded by plywood Eames chairs.

FACING PAGE, TOP
The upstairs master bedroom, with its original tongue-and-groove walls and wraparound windows, incorporates a structural reinforcement on its front-facing wall, a necessity in earthquake-prone country.

FACING PAGE, BOTTOM
In the new powder room downstairs, the framed art is appropriately themed around hair.

bath at the rear of the house was reconfigured to create an expansive kitchen-greatroom space. In the front of the house, the porch was enclosed and combined with the living room, thus bringing light—and a view of the front garden—into a previously dark space.

The updated beach cottage concept continued to evolve when Lucks hired interior designer Valerie Pasquiou, who brought a French Country sensibility to the project with a sophisticated mix of antique, contemporary, and vintage pieces. Added to this were Lucks' own pieces of Asian furniture and her pottery, glass, and art collections.

A few remnants of the original architectural fabric remain, and these are prized. Fragments of vintage beadboard walls and an original staircase are preserved. "If these walls could talk…" says Lucks, reflecting upon the century-long evolution and ultimate transformation of her simple beach cottage.

"I consciously exhaled on visiting Venice where friends had moved in the late '60s. I knew I wanted to live here. Moving to this forward-thinking, close community changed my life completely. I feel safe and at home."
— Linda Lucks

Our Common Ground

Balancing old and new, the
remodeled house retains
the identity of the original
cottage, with its gabled roof
and clapboard siding, and
adds new elements that are
differentiated by form and
materials. The new entry is
visible to the right.

Striking a balance—between old and new,
community and privacy, indoor and outdoor—is the leitmotif for the remodel
and expansion of this small Venice cottage. The
house, built in 1928, had been left to architect
Daniela Rechtszaid by an uncle, and when she
and her husband, Juan José Quintana, a market-
ing consultant, moved in, a modest renovation
was all they envisioned. But when the couple's
need for space outgrew the 700 square feet of
the house—she, working at home, and he, discovering a passion for cooking and entertaining—they realized it was "time to do
something major."

"We sought to keep the identity of the
original cottage, while tying in new forms,"
explained the Argentine-born Rechtszaid. She
retained the gabled façade, with its character-
defining wood siding, and then built upward to
create a second story, sheathing the new
spaces in a smooth stucco finish and introducing a contemporary design sensibility to the
mix. She also made key changes to the circulation, moving the entrance to the side, inserting
a staircase near the new front door, and combining ground-floor back rooms to accommo-

date a large kitchen-dining-living area that
opens to the back. Construction spanned nine
months, beginning in 2000.

Next, a collaboration with landscape architect Russ Cletta brought the garden into focus
with zones that extend living spaces to the outside. To the rear, graciously proportioned seating areas, reading as outdoor rooms, mirror
adjacent interior spaces. The front yard
becomes another landscaped room, its water
feature acting as a counterpart to the fire pit at
the back. Lush plantings—some of them edi-
ble—move through and surround the garden.
These include wisteria, tropical fruit trees, and
hoja santa—gestures to the flora of Quintana's
native Mexico—and contribute to the sense of
privacy.

The casual, light-filled interior is dominated
by the couple's art collection: contemporary
pieces by young Mexican artists mixed with
lively folk pieces and framed art from a family
collection. Hanging such a large and diverse
collection could pose a problem, but the couple has, through trial and error, created an
underlying structure and pattern to the display—keeping some walls blank to provide

balance so as not to overwhelm. Simple furnishings, including classic modernist pieces mixed with the occasional thrift store find, complete the picture of this unpretentious but well-curated interior.

Inside and out, this is a house made for sharing. There are the frequent gatherings of friends, the meals that Quintana enjoys preparing, the nights seated around the fire pit. "Our house means a lot to us," says Quintana, summing up. "Since the two of us are immigrants, here from different countries, this is our common ground, our place in the world."

"Remodeling our original bungalow was a challenge. We loved the old house, we loved the neighborhood, and we loved our garden. Daniela took the project and designed the new house—respecting, as much as possible, the style, footprint, and the spirit of the original."
— Juan José Quintana

LEFT
The guest room at the front of the house opens to a small deck. Its water feature, Buddha statue, adjacent lounge chairs, and hammock set the tone for quiet relaxation.

RIGHT
The back patio, accessible directly from the living area at the rear of the house, serves as an outdoor room, complete with benches and fire pit. Beyond are the studio and garage.

Modern on the Inside

ABOVE
The entry sequence to this modernized bungalow begins at the front gate, which leads to a sequence of steps and an intermediate terrace to the raised front deck. In lieu of the classic front door, two pairs of French doors encourage an easy flow between indoors and out.

FACING PAGE
The perimeter fence is topped with slatted, transparent elements that provide a measure of privacy, yet still mitigate the sense of enclosure. The white siding on the fence's lower portion extends the vocabulary of the bungalow.

By his own admission, David Ritch is a modernist. When he purchased his 950-square-foot California bungalow in 2005 as a teardown, he was handed a set of plans for a three-story contemporary box, ready to build. But then came a change of mind, and heart. At the urging of a dear friend, and on the advice of a trusted contractor, he took another, closer look, and decided to work with what he had.

"It was the best decision I ever made," declares Ritch, an industrial designer. He became his own client and approached the project as he would any new commission, such as an ergonomic chair or an office workstation. The challenge, as he put it, was to "get everything to fit."

To begin, Ritch established some ground rules: retain the house's original footprint, and preserve the character-defining gabled California bungalow exterior, albeit with some subtle contemporary tweaks. The house required an almost complete restructuring—a new roof, ridge beam, walls, and foundation. Ritch managed to preserve some original elements: roof brackets, fascia boards, the under-eave tongue-and-groove, and the high gable window. But he replaced all doors and windows—retaining the spirit of the old, but with simplified molding and millwork profiles.

A key priority for Ritch was to create continuity between indoors and outdoors—a challenge for a house raised three feet above grade. His solution was to create a front deck that terraces gracefully down to the garden,

ABOVE
A built-in ladder, reading as an architectural element, leads to the loft overlooking the principal living areas. With this simple connection to the core space, the "kids become part of the house."

The dining room and kitchen comfortably coexist with comparable degrees of finish. With its refined lines and subtle textures, the limed-oak cabinetry reads as furniture, avoiding a utilitarian feel. Dining table, benches, and clock were designed by David Ritch. Work on paper by Agustin Garza.

RIGHT
The key move in shaping the interior space was opening the ceiling and walls in the front portion of the house to create a generous volume for the core living spaces. Strategically placed skylights further enhance the feeling of spaciousness.

LEFT
Small bedrooms and bathrooms cluster at the back portion of the house. The high awning windows in the master bedroom afford privacy, light, and air. A new skylight throws additional light into the small space. Seascape painting by Victor Hugo Zayas.

RIGHT
Do-it-yourself wall paintings bring a playful expressionism to one of children's bedrooms.

Small tiles unify the wall, shower, and ledge surfaces in this diminutive bathroom, enlarging the sense of space.

Two cantilevered decks with intermediate steps provide a graceful transition from the garden level up three feet to the floor level of the house. A fire pit and seating occupy the smaller of the two decks.

designed as a living space in its own right. Indeed, the bungalow has no classic front door, the entry sequence beginning, intentionally, at the front gate. "Upon entering the garden," he notes, "you've entered the house."

Inside, Ritch employed careful space-planning to utilize every inch. He began by opening up the ceiling at the front of the house, thus creating a generous volume to bring the core living spaces—kitchen, living, and dining room—into one area. This, in turn, created an opportunity for a loft space toward the rear, accessed from the core by a built-in ladder—almost like a tree house, to the delight of his children. Three small bedrooms and two baths occupy the back portion of the house, with storage, cabinets, and built-ins inserted at every opportunity. Ritch introduced skylights where feasible, expanding the sense of space. He also took advantage of the house's original shape, with its jogs along the perimeter, to preserve its natural ventilation: all rooms have windows on two sides.

"Our house feels very full of life, very communal," says Ritch, "yet it manages to balance the open, common areas with private space—a quality that's important to me and my family." This balancing act extends to the design of the house itself—a modernist bungalow, wrapped in traditional garb.

"The design of my Venice bungalow is focused inward, with very well-defined vignettes and boundaries, in a controlled environment. Here, space is at a premium, and we are challenged to reduce the amount of stuff we retain, which, in the end, can be very liberating. My small house has forced me to reevaluate my priorities."
— David Ritch

Eclectic Fantasy

Abbot Kinney Boulevard, in the
heart of Venice, sports an eclectic
mix of boutiques, antique shops,
art galleries, and restaurants.

Mosaic Tile House

In a near-perfect convergence of life and art, the Mosaic Tile House, as it's widely known, embodies the exuberant partnership of Cheri Pann and Gonzalo Duran over nearly two decades.

The couple has transformed a small, nondescript 1940s house, complete with white picket fence, into an eye-popping artwork—an ambitious project not for the faint of heart—channeling Rodia's Watts Towers, Antonio Gaudí, La Maison Picassiette, and the colors of Mexico all at once. As with life, it is a work in progress.

The vision for the house evolved slowly, beginning modestly, with the bathroom (according to Duran), or possibly the front yard

LEFT
Every surface of the Mosaic Tile House is fair game, from the entry gate through the garden, and into the house itself. Cheri Pann makes the tiles, and Gonzalo Duran sets them in combination with found objects, often creating free-form sculptural elements in the process.

ABOVE
Patterns dance upon fields of color, and organic shapes undulate along surfaces, both flat and sculptural. The work continues along the sides of the house, on fences, and into the alleyway behind.

The kitchen, open to the entry vestibule beyond, is the showpiece of the home's interior, and gives the term "kitchen remodel" new meaning. Additional layers of whimsy include hooks used as drawer and door pulls, and a special perch for hanging bananas.

Colorful functional pieces created by Cheri Pann stack on the tile-encrusted shelving.

(counters Pann). No matter. The artist couple—both trained as painters and potters—entered into the perfect collaboration: Pann makes and decorates the tiles, and Duran creates sculptural forms and embellishes the surfaces. For Duran, it was a chance to put into practice something that had fascinated him as a child—the honored tradition of tile work and artisan craft from his native Mexico. Pann, for her part, brought her visual experiences, including travels to Spain and France, to bear, noting that "Gonzalo has been able to translate these diverse inspirations to our Venice home."

All surfaces are fair game: walls, ceilings, cabinets, countertops, and furniture, inside and out. The colorful, textured tapestry features not

In this view from the entry vestibule, brightly painted walls become the backdrop for Duran's guitar paintings and Pann's canvases.

only Pann's tile, broken and set by Duran, but also found objects and other castoffs, as in the Beanie Baby wall, surely the only one of its kind. "I don't exactly plan the shapes, but I approach each new project afresh and let it flow from there," says Duran, commenting on his creative process.

Sometimes, color is eschewed for the reflective surface of broken white tiles and mirror shards on ceilings, and several as-yet unadorned walls are boldly painted, serving as foils for the couple's colorful canvases. Outside, the yard is an evolving sculptural fantasy. With its tiled walls, seating, pergolas, and pathways along which fruit trees thrive, it is a gift to the street.

"Our project has grown because of our community," says Pann. "Their enthusiasm has inspired us to do more." Neighbors bring broken pottery, teapots and the like, while children delight in bringing old toys to contribute to this ever-changing artwork—one small child declaring, "This is even better than Disneyland." Even babes-in-arms, when brought into the house, grow silent and wide-eyed, clearly aware that they are in a place like no other, according to Pann. "The house brings out the best in people," she says with satisfaction. "It makes them feel happy."

"What started as a weekend project has developed into a lifetime love affair. My wife, Cheri Pann, makes the tiles and I break and mosaic them onto surfaces and forms that I create… With the encouragement and involvement of the community, and the donation of shards of pottery and glass, cement, toys, and found objects, we have created a celebration of the creative spirit." —Gonzalo Duran

An Artist's Canvas

When artist Gilah Yelin Hirsch speaks about her home, it is a conversation about a creative process combined with a spiritual journey that has shaped her intensely personal retreat for living and work over the course of several decades. "I consider this house," says Hirsch, "as my biggest work of art."

The house defies traditional labels for a small domestic space—it is neither cottage nor bungalow in the usual sense of the word. Hirsch took a run-down duplex, built in 1904 by two citrus farmers, and connected the two units to create a single home, tightly organized within 1,500 square feet.

LEFT
Behind a perpetually blooming landscape, an early-twentieth-century duplex has been transformed into a private retreat for an artist. A stairway leads to an added studio space above the garage.

ABOVE
A private garden contains a naturally self-sustaining pond that requires no maintenance. Each stone was hand-selected for pattern and form. The large rock was positioned to be fully illuminated at high noon, thus acting as a sundial.

LEFT
An intensely personal environment of rich colors, materials, and forms, bathed in the glow from the skylights above, lends a sense of shelter and mystery to the living areas of the home, including the "pit" room, a favorite place for guests, seen at the front. Paintings are by Gilah Yelin Hirsch.

BELOW
In the office space, world cultures converge in art, artifacts, and furnishings. Original Batchelder fireplace tiles date to the earliest years of the house.

"At the beginning, I was guided by 'what if' thinking," she says, referring to an intuitive, organic process that evolved incrementally as budget and circumstance allowed. What emerged was a sequence of richly embellished spaces that unfolds as a spiral, the movement through which Hirsch describes as a form of meditation. It seems fitting for an artist whose quest is inspired by the rhythms and substance of nature.

She has filled the house with infusions of color and materials, furnishings and art—always with an eye to the organic and the hand-

169

LEFT
Beyond the compact, tightly organized kitchen, the west-facing stained glass windows in the "pit" room create a mandala-like pattern at the summer solstice. This feature, along with others in the house and garden, were designed to synchronize with natural cycles.

BELOW
Light from above bathes the small dining nook. Redwood board-and-batten walls are by woodworker Bill McLeod, whose custom work is found throughout the house.

crafted. Stained glass adorns window openings, and nautilus shells embellish walls and ceilings. Fourteen different kinds of hardwood, each piece selected by Hirsch for its anthropomorphic qualities, are incorporated into custom-made walls, cabinetry, and built-ins. A series of well-placed skylights illuminates the previously dark house, and also provides a special sense of the sky and nature above—the street view offering little to inspire.

A bent redwood arch defines a bed
loft that incorporates 20 linear feet
of rolling closets and drawers under
the bed platform, built by Bill
McLeod. A skylight overhead
provides views of palm trees, birds,
and sky.

"Everything in my home has been designed
with intention," says Hirsch. There are references to natural cycles. A window above
frames the full moon. The brightly colored
"spectrum windows" face due west and create
a mandala-like pattern at the summer solstice.
Outdoors, she built a small pond that is a self-
sustaining ecosystem, requiring no maintenance. Even the rocks were vetted for pattern,
shape, and color, the largest serving as a sundial, carefully placed to be fully illuminated at
high noon.

Hirsch, also a professor of art, frequently
welcomes visitors to her home, and she has
created seating areas, both indoors and outside, where people can congregate. Yet she is
the first to point out that the house contains
no single central gathering space, "kind of like
L.A.," Hirsch wryly observes. One might venture to carry the analogy a bit further—to sug-
gest that, like the city, this intensely layered
home continues to provoke and inspire, as a
place for both discovery and revelation.

*"I do believe that my house is a living entity. Not
only is it rich in natural materials, but it has a
definite vibration. One feels differently on
entering… In creating a painting a moment
arrives when the image begins to reveal itself.
Similarly a deeply considered house: at a certain
point, all the dedicated elements begin to merge,
a unique personality is born, and it too begins to
breathe on its own."* — Gilah Yelin Hirsch

Good Karma

The story of how Phoebe Larmore found and bought her cottage, nestled on a Venice walk street, begins in serendipity and ends in sweetness. In serendipity: when the seller, once an aspiring writer, recognized Larmore, a literary agent then based in New York, from a past encounter in that city, prompting the seller to declare, "Nothing would please me more than if the house were yours." And, following the successful transaction, a moment of sweetness: a bottle of homemade fig jam, waiting for Larmore, the proud new owner, the day of her move.

"In the early 1980s, I traded one bohemian community for another," Larmore recalls of her

Banks of roses surround the front deck of this 1940s cottage, its gable accented with a vintage hubcap. In the front garden, a pergola becomes a framework for a screen of greenery, laced with cascades of bougainvillea and offering a sense of privacy and shelter from the walk street beyond.

LEFT
The living room offers an eclectic mix of cottage comfort and rich-toned Eastern opulence. The master bedroom is visible beyond.

BELOW
Dining and living areas flow together between enclosed front porch and hearthside. Phoebe Larmore switches the rooms seasonally, moving seating to the front of the house for spring and summer garden viewing. At the same time, slipcovers are changed from gold velvets to white embossed cottons.

move from Greenwich Village to Venice, and the purchase, a few years later, of this "sweet home that gives expression to my Virginia small-town-girl roots."

The house, built in 1942—late by Venice standards—appealed to Larmore. She loved the cozy living spaces, and there was room to accommodate her home office needs. Yet the house needed work, inside and out. She tamed the overgrown hedges surrounding the property, while retaining the "secret garden" feel to the place. She added a front deck, extending

the cottage's footprint, and then proceeded to renovate the enclosed front porch to create a generous, light-filled anteroom. This move resulted in an easy flow of space at the front of the house, allowing for flexibility of use by season. Living room and dining room switch places twice a year so that summer days feature the garden flowers and winter evenings can be spent fireside at the cottage's heart.

Deep, rich, jewel-toned colors permeate the home, on walls, furniture, and accessories. Inspiration comes from such diverse sources as the paintings of Matisse, the fabrics of India, and the rich earth-toned palette of Tuscany. Principal rooms contain a sense of an altar, and small Buddha figures preside, evidence of a meditative practice whose presence is felt even by the casual visitor. Tucked throughout the house are family antiques and memorabilia, including a small Civil War–era chair and table used by Larmore's grandfather. Walls are adorned with assemblages by life-partner artist-musician Orville Stoeber, who uses objects and discards found locally to construct whimsical, colorful pieces that embody the spirit of Venice.

Shortly after Larmore found her house, a friend described it as a "force field," and time has proven this to be the case. Here, Larmore has managed to integrate the many threads of her life, passions, and commitments.

"The Venice community is full of people of passion and creativity, individuals who place a premium on freedom of expression. The moment I arrived, I recognized that these were the people of 'my tribe.'" — Phoebe Larmore

FACING PAGE, TOP
The walls of the kitchen, adjacent to the living room area, echo the colors in the vintage tile countertops. On the wall, an old ironing board, stenciled with doilies, by Orville Stoeber.

FACING PAGE, BOTTOM
At the rear of the house is Larmore's "purple cave"—a color she associates with strength and spirituality. Closets have been converted to golden niches for a desk and daybed. Painted ironing board by Orville Stoeber.

ABOVE
The den is all about comfort and cocooning, with an oversized sofa opposite the media cabinet.

Casitas

Beginning in the 1920s, small houses in the Spanish-Mediterranean Revival style began to appear among the eclectic mix of Venice cottages and bungalows.

A Curatorial Eye

A deeply personal home bears witness to the life and the passions of its owner. Such is the 1920s Spanish bungalow of Marla C. Berns, an art museum director. Whether in her collections of ethnic art, in the paintings, prints, and photographs that adorn her walls, or in the furnishings—from high to humble—there is narrative and meaning in the lively tapestry of form, function, and color that flows throughout her house and garden.

Berns bought the 1,250-square-foot home in 2002, drawn to a reconfigured floor plan that offered a pleasing flow for living and entertaining, as well as a yard that held great, if as yet unrealized, potential.

She began inside, painting the walls white over the previous purple, and then seeking out

LEFT
A symphony of color and form marks the entrance to this renovated Spanish bungalow from the 1920s. The horizontal lines of decorative tiles, echoing the rhythms of the roof tiles, are punctuated by colorful potted plants and the vertical tracery of spikes of kangaroo paws.

ABOVE
The enclosed front garden features an intimate seating area and one of a collection of folk muffler men.

LEFT
A treasured gourd collection from Africa and the Pacific celebrates the humble object, and demonstrates how utilitarian objects can be transformed creatively.

The play of vibrant color, pattern, and form against a backdrop of white walls animates the living room. A monoprint by Sam Messer hangs over the sofa.

RIGHT
Kitchen and dining area function as one contiguous space. Saltillo tile flooring knits the principal living area together. On the dining room walls, a watercolor by Ethel Berns, and over the sideboard, a mixed media by Moussa Tine. Color accents are provided by a South African wire basket, one of a collection, and an African runner that echoes the intense blue of the area rug.

delicately-proportioned furnishings for the rooms. "Scale is the key to a harmonious interior," she observes. Thus, a diverse mix of pieces—what Berns calls "eclectic modern"—graces the house. Furniture from the 1950s and 1960s, including several rare, classic pieces by the late California designer Paul Tuttle, a onetime dear friend, mix comfortably with flea market finds and vintage and family pieces.

A view of the living room toward the front yard, with its intense green stucco wall, highlights the complementary color palette of reds and greens that enlivens the spaces of the house, inside and out. Chairs and table are by Paul Tuttle.

FACING PAGE, TOP
The living room fireplace is the focal point for favorite objects, many field-collected abroad during research and work.

FACING PAGE, BOTTOM
Making an asset out of a difficult backyard condition, Berns and landscape designer April Palmer retained the existing concrete, first cutting out a perimeter for a planting bed, then painting the surface an intense color. Further defining the space is a stucco banquette, built against the garage, with an overhead trellis.

Yet it is the collections that grab the eye, with their form, texture, and color, and most of all, the stories behind them. Berns, an art historian, field-collected many of the pieces during her years of research and work abroad. She notes, "I am attracted to the humble object, and to the creativity of people adapting simple materials." She points to her African gourd collection—an example of the creative transformation of a utilitarian object. "People all over the world have adapted the gourd to all kinds of uses," she explains, and the systems for ornamentation are different from village to village, and culture to culture.

The thread of personal meaning continues with art by friends and family, including paintings by her mother. There is also the delight factor—the colors, shapes, and textures of crafts, decorative pieces, and textiles collected simply for the pure pleasure of the objects themselves. "I am an eclectic collector," she says. "If something appeals, I'll buy it and find a place for it."

The playful use of bright hues indoors inspired the color outside—this time, on a larger, more dramatic scale. With the help of landscape designer April Palmer and colorist Joe Nicoletti of Chameleon Paint Works, Berns has transformed her small front and back gardens into boldly colored outdoor spaces. Here, the vivid palette of Luis Barragán's Mexico meets the creative energy of Venice, California. To this, Berns adds a dash of the folk—a sculpture here, an object there—to make the place uniquely her own.

"I enjoy the openness of my small home's renovated floor plan. I spend much of my time sitting in my dining room—at the computer— looking out into the rooms that surround it, which are filled with the objects that bear witness to my life. I am a collector of things that reflect my interests, experiences, and relationships, and I delight in having them around me." — Marla C. Berns

Renovated Spanish Bungalow

"Everyone who comes here says the house is 'you,'" says Erik Joule of his renovated Spanish bungalow on one of Venice's coveted walk streets. To begin with, there is the gateless front yard, a sign of welcome to the steady flow of visitors—both local and from around the globe—who count themselves among Joule's wide circle of friends. Then there is the house itself: authentic in feel with a fashion-forward edge—an apt characterization of Joule himself, an executive with an international action sportswear company.

Joule bought the 1920s bungalow, built by a silent movie star, in 2001, and lived in it for more than four years before embarking on the

LEFT
The controlled color palette of this drought-adaptive garden designed by Laurel Stutsman complements the expanded 1920s Spanish bungalow that it frames. The front yard is gateless, a gesture of welcome to visitors.

ABOVE
An oversized oil jar fountain becomes a focal point in the play of greens and plant forms.

189

remodel. He wanted to be certain he was doing right by the house. With designer Michael Vukusik, he began by inventorying all of the house's original features to ensure their preservation, and then he worked around them. He also was determined to use local resources, artists, and artisans to bring character and a sense of local color and culture to the house. The biggest change: the second-story master suite addition, open to the front and back for wonderful light, vistas, and cross breezes. The biggest challenge: pouring the new foundation, which involved careful excavation and "surgically inserting a new one."

The house has a comfortable, stylish, and spontaneous air, where color and form lend interest and excitement. Vintage Mid-Century pieces mix it up with custom furniture and fixtures designed and fabricated in Venice. Joule is particularly pleased with the "organic" bathrooms built by craftsman Chris Buzzell, featuring handmade tiles and artisan plaster troughs that remind him of the house of his childhood in the south of France.

"It took me a full year to feel at home again," confesses Joule, speaking of the move back once the remodel was complete. "It was the shock of the new, combined with the more spacious environment—the change from 1,100 square feet to 1,750 square feet—that took some adjustment." The sustainable landscaping, designed by Laurel Stutsman, was key to the house's new identity. The front yard engages with the public, acting as the point of connection to the community, while the backyard offers a different, greener, more private experience.

"I do love the juxtaposition of public and private, and the idea of discovery," says Joule. Because he travels constantly for his work, he declares himself fortunate to have this place as home base, observing that "a house should be your space—a great place to land."

FACING PAGE, TOP
Mid-Century meets Spanish Revival
in this view toward the living room
from the dining room, with its
Nakashima table and Paul McCobb
chairs

FACING PAGE, BOTTOM
Bathrooms feature handmade tiles
and custom plaster troughs,
inspired by childhood memories
from France and made by local
craftsman Chris Buzzell.

ABOVE
The lily pad sofa by Elizabeth Paige
Smith and Mid-Century glassware
are among the many items in the
house sourced locally, from Venice-
based designers and vintage shops.

"In our culture, I think we have become accustomed to 'bigger being better' and 'more is more.' However, I do find that an intimate space tends to allow you to express yourself more directly. There is warmth that comes from human-scaled spaces, whether it is in a city or a house."
— Erik Joule

The den is all about color, playful and uninhibited. Throughout the house, casement windows, absent any window coverings, frame garden views.

The stairway leading to the added second floor features an organic wall sculpture of palm frond stems and a painting by Jennifer Wolf.

Viewed through an arched doorway, the small breakfast nook adjacent to the kitchen, with its view of the front garden, accommodates a vintage Murano glass pendant and a Mid-Century dinette set.

Venice Caliente

In her landscape design practice, April Palmer is guided by reverence for place, so when she found a small house in Venice that had been owned by a Mexican-American family for many decades, she was inspired to tread lightly. The *casita*, as she calls it, was built in the 1930s as a single-room cottage and grew over the years with small additions. Throughout these incremental changes, it retained the spirit of casual informality that spoke to its particular history.

She wanted to preserve that spirit. "I didn't want to impose an artificial vision on this house," she says. Instead, she "brought Mexico to Venice," introducing vivid, saturated colors to the exterior and garden spaces of the small

LEFT
Vivid, saturated colors and bold plantings in the front courtyard of Palmer's casita bring the spirit of Mexico to Venice.

ABOVE
Blues and purples pop against the complementary hue of the terra cotta walls.

195

LEFT
In the main living space of the house, white walls form the backdrop for a colorful, casual collection of furniture, art, textiles, and objects that reflects Palmer's passion for travel. Paintings were gifts from family members.

BELOW
The view from the living room to the front entryway frames the colorful front gate. The coffee table holds carved painted wood animals and black pottery from Oaxaca. The vintage toy fire engine belongs to Palmer's grandson.

walled compound with paint, furnishings, and accessories. New plantings that would also be at home in Mexico renewed the garden with color and bold form. The large, rustic brick barbeque, a holdover from the previous residents, continues to serve as a focal point for the informal, spontaneous gatherings that Palmer enjoys with her close Venice community.

Inside, Palmer took a somewhat different approach, using white walls as the backdrop for colorful furnishings, art, and collections. "I enjoy primitive, indigenous pieces with a sophisticated sense," she says of the objects she has gathered in her travels to Mexico and Central

197

LEFT
Painted birdcages, used as wall décor, enliven a corner of the front garden.

RIGHT
Casual hospitality is the watchword in Palmer's garden, a place for frequent gatherings. California pottery inspired by the colors of the Southwest graces the table, surrounded by *equipale* chairs from Mexico.

America. She has mixed this up with art reflecting a more traditional sensibility—American and European paintings, some handed down from family—resulting in a relaxed, assured layering of furniture and accessories.

Palmer, trained as a painter, and with a career that has spanned the fields of fashion and advertising, now finds great satisfaction in her work with landscapes. She has carried that passion to shaping her own domestic environment. "My home and my garden are where I start," she says, "to integrate an awareness of our place in the universe into the natural order of things."

"I love the Mexican architectural and color sensibility. My old bungalow was previously the home of a Mexican family of gardeners. It gave me a great canvas to play with colors, fill with the crafts and art I've collected in my travels, and create lush gardens inside the surrounding wall for my own Mexican-style casita." — April Palmer

Stage Set

All the world's a stage: a pair
of weathered antique doors,
topped with a pergola, offers
a sense of drama at the entry
to a Venice cottage garden.

A Magic Kingdom

The adventure begins just inside the front gate with the sound of water—a gentle meditative fountain, signaling, already, a change of pace. Overhead, scores of colorful, ornate glass globe lamps adorn the trees. Connecting a row of three small cottages, one behind the other on a narrow lot, is a series of decks and walkways populated with whimsically arranged vignettes of found objects, large and small. We have entered a magic kingdom where the combined passion for collecting, color, and community plays itself out in the exuberant home of Scott Mayers.

"I use every inch of my house to live, love, and entertain in," says Mayers, who bought the

A series of decks and walkways connects three small cottages, where vignettes of found objects may be discovered at every turn. Overhead, a collection of two hundred hanging glass globes, specially wired for exterior use, provide visual candy during the day and illumination at night.